Beginners Guide for
I.S.S.R. Shiloh Shepherd Owners

Steve Mekkelsen Madden

Beginners Guide for
I.S.S.R. Shiloh Shepherd Owners

Outskirts Press, Inc.
Denver, Colorado

Shiloh Shepherd™ is a trademark of the International Shiloh Shepherd™ Registry.

The International Shiloh Shepherd™ Registry, Inc. is the only registry authorized to recognize a dog as a Shiloh Shepherd™. The I.S.S.R. was formed to protect the public from purchasing a dog falsely represented to be a Shiloh Shepherd™ and to protect the genetic future of the breed. Thus, only dogs having a certificate of registration issued by the I.S.S.R. may be considered a Shiloh Shepherd™.

Additional information can be obtained from the breed founder's "Tina M. Barber" daughter at: http://www. shilohshepherds.org.

The opinions expressed in this manuscript are solely the opinions of the author and do not represent the opinions or thoughts of the publisher. The author has represented and warranted full ownership and/or legal right to publish all the materials in this book.

Preface

Thank you for purchasing this book. There are obviously many dog books out there to choose from for training, handling and showing dogs of all breeds. This book is different; as I will be talking about what it is like to own and raise a Shiloh Shepherd™. While some of the topics discussed can be applied to other breeds, the primary purpose of this book is focused on I.S.S.R. Shiloh Shepherds™.

It is important to identify right up front, that our breed; Shiloh Shepherds™ are so unique, so different, so smart, so loving and so attentive, I am confident by the end of this book, you too will want one, or more as we did. ☺

This book is written to keep it interesting and informative and to provide guidance from day one of receiving your Shiloh Puppy for potty training, basic training, handling and showing your Shiloh Shepherds™ and so much more.

I have written this as a beginner's guide, not an all exclusive or everything and anything guide that can come with owning a dog of any breed. It is limited, but meant to be informative for the beginner only.

Legal Information

The author and publisher do not guarantee any method or advice provided in this book to work 100% of the time. As with any book or advice provided, it is up to the reader/owner to determine what is best for his/her dog given the information provided. I provided the details from our personal experiences and what has worked for us. Results can vary from dog to dog and breed to breed.

Consult with your professional dog trainer/handler for more information for techniques mentioned which may not be working for your situation.

Consult with your veterinary doctor for any/all medical advice and treatments mentioned before trying them yourself. As with any medical condition, it is your responsibility to ensure you have an accurate diagnosis before treatment is administered.

All medical information provided by other sources are copyrighted by those sources. The author and publisher do not assume any liability for any medical information to be accurate for every situation. Consult with your veterinary doctor before taking any action.

Acknowledgements

We would like to say thank you to Tina Barber who was the breed founder. Without her decades of hard work, diligence, persistence and dedication to making this breed the best possible, we would not have the fine breed we have today. Her daughter, Lisa Barber continues on with her mother's life's work. We miss you Tina, may your road to the life thereafter be as rewarding as the life with us.

I would also like to thank my wife Sherri from the bottom of my heart ,for without her many years of research into dog breeds, finding Tina's dogs, her continuous years of study to become an I.S.S.R. Shiloh Shepherd Licensed Breeder and diligence in learning all she can about the breed, genetics, history and other Shilohs in the world. Otherwise, it would not be possible to write this book!

A special thank you goes out to Keith Walker - a local professional dog trainer. Keith gave us the foundation training with Mali (our first Shiloh) all the way through to Advanced Training. We then applied the knowledge learned from Keith for Mali's training to the other three Shilohs we have and any other dog that we come across that needs that extra training when appropriate. ☺

Thank you to everyone on the Shiloh Shepherd™ Forum who provided input into the content and other materials to make up this book.

Thank you to Maria Crossman for also taking the time reading, editing, practicing and providing valuable input and much needed edits, into this book to ensure our readers understand exactly what we've provided. ☺

Medical conditions and references - the source of this information is from our personal experiences our veterinary doctors, from www.PetMD.com, www.EntirelyPets.com, Alaska State Public Health Lab, The CDC-DPDx (http://www.dpd.cdc.gov/dpdx/HTML/Image_Library.htm for roundworms) and Cuyahoga Falls Veterinary Clinic, Inc. (http://fallsvetclinic.com for demodex) which provides a list of common medical conditions and their treatments. As with any medical issue, seek the advice from your veterinary doctor immediately when you notice changes in your dogs' behaviors. Also, keep your breeder informed of any and all medical issues with your dog so that they can keep track of them. Having a comprehensive list of genetic faults and medical conditions is important to ensure future breedings minimize the risk of new offspring.

Table of Contents

CHAPTER 1

What is a Pack Leader?

Be Pack mindful

This starts with the first day you get your puppy. It is important to establish rules as soon as you take responsibility of your dog. Dogs work in packs and in packs there is a leader or alpha dog. This alpha dog is almost always a female when you have both male and female. There will always be a predominant alpha figure in your pack and you, the human, should always be the alpha of your pack.

What happens when you don't take control of your pack? Complete chaos will come in your home and it will be harder to get it under control as the dog ages. Your dog will bark in the house, jump on you and strangers, go potty in places where he/she should not, chew on furniture and destroy your way of living! This is obviously not what you asked for so we'll help you get started.

Being the Pack Leader

What does it mean to be the Pack Leader? Simply stated, it means you control every aspect of what you want your dog to do. Obviously, there are some restrictions but throughout this book we'll cover almost 2 dozen commands that we use regularly so that we enforce positive behaviors. Being the pack leader means that you will provide a command or instruction to your puppy/dog and they will respond accordingly. Your dog will try to please you, so it is up to you to constantly challenge and allow your puppy to grow up to be an intelligent member of your pack.

Dogs are pack animals, just like wolves, coyotes and hyenas. Wild pack animals live together in family groups which have an Alpha leader and lower ranking members. Domestic dog packs, like their wild relative live much the same way with an Alpha leader and lower ranking members, neither of these groups are a democracy, but are more like a dictatorship.

Every member of the pack knows exactly what its rank is within the pack from the highest member to the lowest ranking member. Pups are born seeming to genetically understand this concept. At about 4 weeks of age, they begin playing their own version of pack hierarchy within the whelping box. It is at this age when they are actively playing, biting, growling, knocking each other over. The pups that are the strongest and the loudest rank highest in the whelping box hierarchy.

Needless to say Mom is the Alpha paws down. After all, she provides the food, the warmth, and the protection; as well as, doles out and real corrections if any. As the pups grow older it is mom who will show her teeth or growl when she does not want to share her food with the pups or has been climbed on, one too many times. She demonstrates the true leadership the pups need and teaches them the first things they need to learn in the wild world out of the whelping box.

When you bring your puppy home, you need to establish yourself as the new pack leader. A pack leader does not mean you are, mean, bossy or dominate over your new pup. On the contrary, a pack leader is calm, confident, firm and always fair. There is no need to yell or lose your temper. A puppy has far better hearing than you or I and like children they have short attention spans and selective hearing. Like children they often need redirection.

You have just brought home your new puppy and up until this point, it has had only whelping box hierarchy with its mother as the Alpha and its littermates as pack members, biting and growling for the most part its main ways of interacting with its pack. The first day or so, it might need to settle in, but then your sweet pup may turn into a shark, all teeth and you are its favorite sport. Your pup has accepted you as its new pack member and is trying to interact with you the same way it did with its littermates with biting, growling, chasing and biting some more. Your pup is trying to find out its rank in this new pack and when you think about it this way, it is really quite logical.

Now it is your job to help this "shark" puppy to find its rank, gently, right at the bottom. You are its new pack leader and it is your time to lead. Many people become frustrated at this time in a puppy's life as it takes time for a puppy to understand and those teeth are so sharp! Stick with it and I promise you the pup will learn.

Some people overreact and others ignore problems, which arise when they have puppies, either of these would be ill advised. Overreacting could cause your pup to grow up as a shy dog and ignoring issue can leave a dog thinking it is in control.

Getting Started

Before we get started, we're going to assume a few things. Your new "dog" is a puppy about 8-14 weeks old and you have no clue what to do other than what your breeder gave you for information on feeding, etc. Most people know dogs need to eat, be taken care of and go potty. What isn't so common is what also goes with all these responsibilities when things don't go as planned. ☺

Feeding your Puppy

Each puppy may have different appetites and or tastes for foods. If you are planning on feeding raw foods (chicken and beef), you must follow the guidelines set forth in your contract on what to feed and on what schedule. When you are unsure when you can change/add something to your puppy's diet, check with your breeder. Puppies should be fed on time and on a regular schedule while they are growing. The breeder will tell you when the puppies are used to eating, so sticking to that schedule is always best. As your puppy gets older, he/she will most likely change their minds when they want to eat and this is normal. Puppies should be fed 3 times a day and can gradually as they get older be moved to twice a day. Our girls are 2+ years old now and they only want to eat once a day and at night. Sometimes they get a snack during the day, but their main meal is at night. This varies from pack to pack and dog to dog.

Puppies generally start out by eating mush food. This is basically, some kibble that came with the breeder which the puppy has been on and is used to, some non-fat yogurt, vitamins and some raw meat mixed into the food (for the protein). You need to start out with some large breed puppy kibble and it is important you start with the same brand as what was given to you by the breeder. This will help prevent diarrhea because of a change in diet. You can almost always count on some diarrhea so you need to keep an eye on it especially when changing the food they eat.

If your puppy does have troubles with a changing diet, you can add to their food some cooked rice, fresh pumpkin or real pumpkin in the can. The yogurt helps the puppies digest all the foods. Just a tablespoon of each is fine, same with the low-fat Yogurt.

When you want to introduce a new kibble, it is best to mix it 50/50 with the old kibble so the puppy's digestive system can handle it better.

Some brands we have used are: Nutro Natural Choice, Ultra and Max Large Breed Puppy/Adult, California Natural and

Canidae. Our dogs are now on Canidae they just love it. What you need to look out for is recalls and when you need to switch brands either because of cost, quality or safety reasons for your pet. Always check with the FDA recall website for latest and up to the minute details on pet foods which may be recalled. See Chapter 14, Pet Food Recall List for more information.

When in doubt, check with your breeder or post your question(s) on the Shiloh Shepherd™ Community Forum / Learning Center if you need more information about what to feed your puppy or adult dogs. There is a website link you can visit in Chapter 14.

Potty Schedule

Puppies don't have a large bladder so they will be going to potty more frequently until they get older. Most puppies already come to you paper trained, so you just need to pick a spot for them to go until you determine what their schedule is for when they need to go potty out doors.

Make a note when they first start and then take them out every hour and gradually increase the time as they get a couple weeks older. Eventually, you'll be able to go 4-6 hours in between potty times. Of course, there are always those dogs that have weak bladders and just can't hold it. ☺

Potty training a dog is very similar to potty training a child. It takes time and a lot of patience and when they are ready, they are ready. The sooner you introduce paper training, the easier the transition to outdoors.

One thing that works pretty well (at least for us), is when you know you are going out for an hour or two, don't put down any papers and when you return let your puppy out for potty and praise them for holding it. You'll know when to start this routine - typically when the paper is dry when you have left and re-turned home. You can gradually (each week) increase the time and eventually not having papers on the floor and having your puppy completely house-broken / potty trained. Remember to praise your puppy each and every time they potty outdoors!! This is key to their learning and success.

CHAPTER 2

How to train your Shiloh

Sixteen basic training commands

We start with the sixteen basic commands which you will want to teach your new puppy. This list of commands will grow as we progress through the rest of this book. You can start on day one of receiving your puppy, as he/she may already understand a few of them. It's important they understand and learn, you now are the pack leader and they take instructions from you. All puppies from our Kennels are trained the same way for consistency.

Command Overview

1. Sit	7. Release	13. Watch
2. Stand	8. No	14. Nose
3. Down	9. Wait	15. Not Yours / Leave it
4. Stay	10. Left	16. Here
5. Come	11. Right	
6. Off	12. Back	

Each command is described briefly below. We will get into the specific details of each command shortly.

Sit - The dog needs to sit and remain calm submissive while you do what you need to do. Do not however, expect your dog to sit very long, as puppies have short attentions spans. They will sit awaiting your next command for a few moments.

Stand - This is a very useful command which you'll use more in Show rings, but is very useful when you have a sitting dog and you want them to stand and get ready for the next command or get ready to go somewhere.

Down - The dog should be lying down in either an alert position (lying but not on their side) or just resting (on their left or right side). Down does not mean to Stop jumping, or get off of furniture, it means lie down. If you use this command for more than one thing your puppy or dog will become confused.

Stay - This is one command where you have your dog stay in one spot for an indeterminate period of time. It could be 5 minutes or 20 minutes. Generally, when you put a dog in a Down, they will stay as long as they are told to or until you command them otherwise.

However with a puppy you cannot expect it to stay very long in one position. Do not set it up to fail. Get your puppy to stay for a few seconds and then praise it and/or treat your puppy, slowly increasing the time you have it stay in one place.

Come - The hardest command to teach your dog. It is important that this command NEVER be used in a negative manner or you will have troubles with retrieving your dog when you need to most. Come should always be used in a pleasant and rewarding manner to make your dog come to you, sit in front of you and wait for your command. During training always use a long line so you can reel in your puppy so it can never fail in returning to you.

Off - This command will save your furniture and friends. Don't let your dogs jump on you without explicitly asking for them to do so. After all, these dogs grow to 100+ pounds each and they can very easily knock you over or more seriously injure you if you are not ready for it. Dogs should always have all four paws on the ground. When they jump on things or people when not allowed, simply use the command **OFF** in a serious but firm tone. **Off** is the term used rather than down for jumping up on people or furniture.

Release - This command is used to instruct your dog it is now okay to relax and stand, walk, play or just be themselves. Typically, if you have you dog in a down/stay, you use the Release command to let them know they don't have to stay any longer. It is advisable though, when you use the Release command, you train your dog to come to you when you say it.We have known people to use many words other than re-lease. Some people use words in other languages, for release or have even made up their own words. Whatever word you decide to use, always be consistent in what you decide to do when training your puppy.

No - or a sound indicating you don't like what they are doing (e.g. uh uh) and you want them to stop immediately.

Wait - having your puppy wait before crossing a doorway so you can go first. You are the pack leader, and the pack leader always goes first. Having them wait temporarily while you get the car ready, cross the street or meet another human or dog. For me, this is very important as I have such problems with my balance. All of our dogs had to learn to wait and let me go out of the door first or they would knock me down. Even as young puppies, they had to learn to wait. This is something to consider if you have young children in your home or elderly people, making your pups or large dogs wait and let those who could easily be knocked over go first.

Left - to go to the left, yes dogs will learn left from right. When you walk or run your dog in the park, you need to let them know which direction to go. Steve walks all three girls together holding onto the leash with one hand. It is a small paved walk way shared with people on bikes and he often has to give away the path to the bikers. Having the girls know their left from right has helped a great deal.

Right - to go to the right, yes dogs will learn right from left. When you walk or run your dog in the park, you need to let them know which direction to go. You should see them taking the turns in the park, all three girls out in front of him running as fast as Steve can go, because they could easily go a lot faster. When Steve decides which path they will take he says left or right letting the girls know which one to take.

Back - use this when you need your dog to back up when they are too far ahead of you. It is fun to watch your dog to walk backwards and they do a great job at it. This is one command which can and usually needs repeating in a positive manner.

Watch - This is one of the first commands I taught Mali and it has been one of the most helpful. It is quite simple to teach. Teaching your puppy to watch you and ignore other distractions will make training much easier. This is how to teach your puppy; make sure you are in a quiet place with a high value treat ready. You can begin either sitting or standing in front of your puppy. I sat, as I like to be closer to eye level. When your puppy looks right at you, quickly say to it Watch! Give a treat right away, then praise.

If for some reason your puppy will not look up at you because it is distracted, you can use the treat scent to get its attention. Then bring the treat next to your eye and say Watch! Treat him and praise. You can continue to in this manner until your puppy understands.

It is important your dog does not see the treat first. You want him to look at your eyes and not at the treat. You only give him the treat if he looks at your eyes. Practice this off and on many times during the day, your puppy will learn. Eventually you will be able to hold a treat anywhere and say watch me and your pup will still be able to look at your eyes and not the treat.

Nose - This command we started using because I personally cannot stand counter surfing dogs. It also went in well as a command for my service dog not sniffing things she should not be sniffing. We taught the girls at a young age to keep their noses to themselves with this command. When a pup or dog lifts their nose to my counter to take a sniff at what is there they are corrected with the command nose. They have learned nothing on the counter is theirs until we give it to them. We could leave a roast on the counter with all three girls in the room and not one of them would so much as do more than sniff from the other side of the room.

Not Yours / Leave It - this is a great command to tell your dog to not touch something or leave something behind when you need them too. It is a very important command which could save your dogs life when you don't want them touching something they shouldn't be.

Mali is such a little sneak. One day Steve went to let the girls out and he stopped Mali at the door as her mouth seemed a little out of sorts, a little misshapen. I watched as he asked her what she had in her mouth. She answered him in a muffled voice, Wooo wooo woo. The sides of her lips puffed out on both sides of her face. I tried not laugh because it was then obvious she had something in her mouth she was trying to sneak out of the house.

I came into the kitchen too as I wanted to get a better look. She looked up at me with innocent eyes and paced a little then returned to the door. Steve had since let the other girls out of the house and just Mali, Steve and I were left in the kitchen. Mali stood there now at the door and her innocent eyes were now ridden with guilt, but she still held her mouth closed.

Steve asked her again, "Mali what do you have in your mouth?" she Wooo'd only once this time and then mumbled deep in her chest. I swear she scuffed her paws at imagined sand on the kitchen floor as she rocked back and forth on her front feet. She lowered her head towards the floor, I thought she was going to drop whatever it was but she did not, instead she repositioned it deeper in her mouth. She lifted her head and looked at us almost smiling.

I remember drawing both my lips into my mouth to keep from smiling, but my eyes rolled, then Steve and I looked at each other and both said, "Nice try Mali. Leave it!" Oh my, she was devastated she thought she had fooled us. The look on her face was one of utter shock. Steve said, Leave it again. Mali lowered her head and spit out a raw chicken thigh. YUCK! I exclaimed, where the heck did you hide that! It was a left-over from her dinner last night. I was positive she ate all her dinner. She must have hidden it somewhere, but where she could take it out to burry today.

Here - Is a word we use instead of come when we are not sure we can get the puppy to come. We do not want our dogs to ever fail when we say come during training off lead. We make sure to train in an enclosed area so there is no danger of our puppy escaping into traffic or getting lost. We want to give it a chance to come to us on its own even with all the distractions; so we use the word **HERE** instead of **COME**.

Picking your commands

You now have sixteen basic commands to start with. The key to any command is repetition and consistency. Use these commands only for the purpose implied behind it. If you say **OFF** when you mean **DOWN,** the dog will just be confused and not know what to do. Commands should never have more than one meaning.

Unlike humans where we can distinguish dual meaning words like "write" and "right" or "rose - flower" and "rose - rise", dogs cannot. You are not bound by this book to use the words we chose, you can pick your own as long as you stick with them!

You also do not need to speak the commands in English. Commands can be done in any language and the sign language will just reinforce what you want them to do. Remember however, your puppy may be arriving understanding some commands in English.

As we progress, single commands can turn into sentences when your dog gets used to what it is you are asking of him/her. Just be firm, consistent and repetitive in your commands and you will be amazed at the results. Here are some others.

CHAPTER 3

Command Review

Sitting can be very humbling; even to just show off that pretty new shirt or blending in with the background and pretending to be part of the scenery.

Sit! When you need your dog to sit, say the command with conviction, but not yelling at the dog. It is important you communicate to the dog and not shout or order the dog around especially with soft temperament dogs. We always start training our puppies with both verbal and hand signals right from the start. I have found it so much easier when my dog is across a crowded room and I want it to do something, all I have to do is say its name and sign what I want it to do. In a multiple dog home, this to can be very helpful as well.

Have you ever noticed when you are facing a dog and walk towards them they will instinctively backup when you walk close to them? They will also sit when you have something in your hand and hold it above their head. Find a nutritious dog treat which your dog likes, then get the dog's attention by teasing them for a few seconds with a treat you have in your hand; but not giving it to him/her.Hold the treat just above and in front of their head about 6 inches with your palm turned up and say the word SIT at the same time. Once the dog sits, give them the treat. Repeat this as many times as needed - eventually, you will not even need to say the word, just turn your palm up, and the dog will see the hand sign and know you want them to sit.

If your puppy is a little stubborn and does not sit right away using this method, at the same time you say SIT and hold the treat above their head, gently (not forcefully) press down on their butt to get them to sit. The first time may be the hardest, but you should not have to do this part to many times before they get the hang of it.

Another trick would be to back your puppy into a corner so he would not back up when you bring the treat over its head as the corner would stop it and would have to sit instead in order to see where the treat is.

The idea here is they get a treat when you say a command and show a sign for them to act on. When they know there is something good in it for them, they will just about do it on their own.

Do not repeat commands

It is also important not to repeat the commands. For example, sit Mali sit or sit, sit, sit. This will only bore your dog and make training more difficult. A Shiloh you will end up with will have selective hearing and you will soon be tuned out! These are smart dogs; they think and often learn how to train their owners before you learn how to train them. Have a clear picture in your mind about what you want to do and keep it simple and quick.

Most pups are food motivated. If your pup is, then it is best to practice your training when your dog is hungry and you will most often see positive results. As they get older this will change some and you may have to find other things to motivate them. However, when they are young, food works for most of them quite well.

As they grow a little older, training is easier after a walk or run in the park. The older puppy has released some of their pepped up energy and will be more receptive to your commands.

Getting your dog to stand is probably one of the easiest things you can do. Since in most instances, your dog is already standing right? What happens if your dog wants to sit down when you want him/her to stand? What do you do?

Depending on the size of your dog you may need to kneel down or bend over to do this; reach under their belly and tickle the belly towards the middle and before the hind legs. You can do this as long as you need the dog to be standing.

We will talk more about tickling the belly when we get to showing. Standing is a very important in the show ring, so you'll want to make sure your dog is ready for this as soon as possible.

Sit to Stand - If your dog is sitting and you want him/her to stand, pull the leash towards you gently making the dog move forward and say **Stand.** The dog will automatically go into a stand. Decide what you want to use for a hand sign as well during this process. I use a closed fist (loosely closed) and hold it about 6 inches in front of their face while I say the command **Stand.**

Down to Stand - If your dog is lying down and you want him/her to stand, call the dog by name and say **Come.** You can also use the hand sign of extending your arm straight out and bending the arm at the elbow and pulling inwards to touch your chest. Have the palm touch your chest and then say **Come.**

Once your dog is standing (even if for a moment at first), reward him/her with a dog treat. This promotes good behaviors with rewards.

Down! Now this is the one we all get confused with. Off and Down are not the same. When you want a dog to lie down, then the command is simply **Down.** When you want a dog off your furniture, your lap, your neighbor, then say **Off.**

Once your puppy has learned to sit we can move on to the next position which for some is not quite so easy. Down is a very vulnerable position for a dog and some find it hard to give in to. I find the best way to teach this position is to start at a sitting position. I start by getting the puppy to sit, giving the pup a treat and praise. Next I take a treat and lower it to the floor letting the puppy follow it with its nose; as I do this I say the word down. Sometimes the puppy will drop to the floor right away. If this happens you had better believe I make sure the puppy gets lots of praise. If not, then I draw the treat outwards some, slowly making sure to let the pups have a lick here and there and possibly a nibble until the pup figures out it is best to lie on the floor for its best advantage. All the while, I am saying the word **Down**.

I repeat this exercise quicker each time and with Shilohs, it does not take very many times for them to understand "Down means down" gets a treat. Soon after I am using a hand sign with the treat and my palm facing the floor, just my first finger and thumb holding the treat and Mali hits the floor. The softer ones like Hera wag their tails and wiggle their way down while smiling at me because they know they are going to get something yummy.

You do not need to yell at your pup, a soft Shiloh like Yuki or Hera would melt if you did speak loudly. Some like Mali and Zeus, you might have to be a little firm with but you never need to be a bully or rough as these dogs will learn for the joy of learning and because they want to make you happy.

Stay can be associated with **Sit, Stand** and **Down.** In most cases, you should not need to provide a second command of **Stay** when a dog is Down. It is implied, but in some situations with very active dogs it is okay to remind them to stay down as long as you need them to be. They may eventually even lay their head down or roll to one side. A completely relaxed dog would even let out a huge sigh during this.

However since you are working with puppies, remember they have short attention spans and should not be expected to stay for any longer than a few seconds at a time. As they grow older you can slowly increase their time. Always have them stay when on a leash so you can draw them back to you if they should break their stay.

If you should decide to try and have your dog stay off leash, make sure you are in an enclosed area so they will not have a chance of breaking a stay and accidently running off and into traffic.

The hand sign for this is also very similar to **Stop** with your hands. Hold your hand out with the palm facing the dog about six inches from your pups nose and say **Stay.** That's it, it is that simple. It may also be necessary to repeat every few seconds until the dog understands com-

pletely just how long you mean to stay.

Stay could even be a game to see how long your pup will stay while you go do something with them or get a treat for a special occasion.

Come! Having your dog come back to you is one of the hardest tricks to teach your dog. Some get it from day one and are reliable and will always come. Others will test you to make sure you really mean what you say. Yes, they can behave like an adolescent and try your patience, just be firm and not scold them. Especially with this command!! If you want your dog to come when called by name, it should always, always be a positive experience.

To have your dog come to you, the hand sign is to extend your arm straight out and then bring it straight in and touch your

chest in one motion like you were waving to someone and saying to them come on over here but you are bringing your arm/palm to your chest.

You should practice this at first with the dog on a leash and using the command, hand sign and a treat, say **Come** to the dog and with the hand movement towards your chest pull in on the leash with the hand that is coming inwards. When the dog is pulled towards you, reward your pup and give them a treat.

Rewarding your pup should be as simple as good girl, good boy and patting their head and chest. Making them feel like they have done something so awesome you are so proud of them. This is true for many commands.

Off is the command to use when you do not want your pup jumping on ANYTHING! It does not matter what it is: furniture, a person, a child, car, couch, wall or even another dog. **Off** simply means get off.

If your pup jumps up on you, quickly pull both arms inward to your chest and turn away while saying OFF. You will need to repeat this until they get it. If your dog jumps on someone else, they can do the same or you can pull on the collar and say **Off.** This is one area where you should **NEVER** allow your pup to jump on anything or anyone at anytime without an explicit command to do so. It teaches them an incorrect behavior that says it is okay to jump on you and walk all over you, which is never the intent.

We start out the puppies we raise, right in the kitchen, when they are climbing on the baby gate telling them off when we come over to see them. Each time they climb up to see us, we gently take their feet off the gate and say off and put them back on the floor. It does not take them long to figure it out. The ones on the floor are the ones who are being petted.

Release! When we feed our dogs, beef knuckle bones, we place them on the floor and say leave it and can leave the room without any concern that they will touch or eat the bones. Once we are ready, we give the command **Eat** or **Release** and they go right to the bones!

There are many other commands you can teach your pup, but these are only the basics. Once you and your pup have mastered these, try some new ones. Remember, that commands should be single words. You can also start talking in sentences to your pup once they have mastered the commands. They will pick up the command in the sentence, so it will become more natural for you over time.

No - This is a command when you need to redirect your dog. It can be a simple No or a sound indicating you don't like what they are doing (e.g. uh uh) and you want them to stop immediately.

Wait - When we want our girls to wait for us to go through an open doorway or just stop and wait for us to give them a command to continue, we say wait and hold our hand in front of their face with your palm facing them (like stop) and just say wait. They will learn that wait is a temporary state and they will be able to continue shortly. Wait is not intended to be longer than a few seconds.

Left - Using the command Left will instruct your pack or dog to go in the direction you need them to. When you are jogging or running and you want to go left and cross in front of them, it is very dangerous since your dog is focused on going straight. You need to pull on the leash towards the left and say the command "**Left**" so their head moves to the left and their body will follow. This is very similar to riding a horse when you pull the reins towards the left.

Right - Using the command Right will instruct your pack or dog to go in the direction you need them to. When you are jogging or running and you want to go right and need your dog to follow you, simply pull on the leash towards the right and say the command "**Right**" so their head moves to the right and their body will follow. This is very similar to riding a horse when you pull the reins towards the right.

Back - If your dog ever gets ahead of you and you need them to wait or move back while you progress forward, you can use Wait for them to stop and wait for you to catch up or just say "**Back**" while you stand still and have them move backwards. This teaches the dog you are in command and are the pack leader and they need to back up and wait for you to continue.

Watch - This is one of the first commands I taught Mali and it has been one of the most helpful. It is quite simple to teach. Teaching your puppy to watch you and ignore other distractions will make training much easier. This is how to teach your puppy; make sure you are in a quiet place with a high value treat ready. You can begin either sitting or standing in front of your puppy. I sat, as I like to be closer to eye level. When your puppy looks right at you, quickly say to it Watch! Give a treat right away, then praise.

If for some reason your puppy will not look up at you because it is distracted, you can use the treat scent to get its attention. Then bring the treat next to your eye and say Watch! Treat him and praise. You can continue to in this manner until your puppy understands.

It is important your dog does not see the treat first. You want him to look at your eyes and not at the treat. You only give him the treat if he looks at your eyes. Practice this off and on many times during the day, your puppy will learn. Eventually you will be able to hold a treat anywhere and say watch me and your pup will still be able to look at your eyes and not the treat.

Nose - When a pup or dog lifts their nose to a counter, table or where there may be food or breakables to take a sniff, say the command "**Nose**" and redirect them. As time goes on, the dog will learn what Nose means and will correct itself when you say it.

Not Yours /Leave It is used when you do not want your dog to touch something at that moment or at all. They will learn what it is as time goes on and understand that Leave It means do not touch! This is a simple command to teach and to teach this command you will need two treats to start out. The first treat you place in front of your dog on the floor and say leave it, while in the other hand you show you have another treat for him/her. You want to make sure he/she sees the treat on the floor, but you also need to redirect them to look at the other treat. If your pup leaves the treat on the floor, you reward the pup with the treat in your hand.

Repeat this several times a day and each time moving further away with the second treat so they come to you and leave the one on the floor alone. Do NOT feed the treat to the dog that was on the floor when they are watching, this may just lead to confusion.

Here - This very much like Come but may have a negative action associated with it. Use the command "**Here**" when your dog has gone somewhere, like escaping a fenced in area or gone astray after another animal and needs to return back to you and be corrected. This is only used to tell the dog they did something wrong and you want them to know what they did was wrong and there is a consequence for it. This of course does not mean you beat your dog either. You can talk firmly to the dog and say No or something that fits what it is they did. Come is always used in positive manner where Here is most often used in a negative manner.

Specialized Commands

Medicine! We have even taught our girl Rani "**Medicine**", and she knows to lie down on her side and I can put in eye drops and say **over** and she rolls over and I can do the other eye! Sometimes she just moves her head the opposite way so I can just drop one in.

Other Side - this is used to get Rani to turn over (roll over) to her other side so we can do the other eye. She learned getting medicine is a positive experience. She gets eye drops to help with the runny eyes she had with the allergies and she gets to spend time in the living room and gets tons of praise for being a good girl!

Inspection! You'll love this one! I've taught the girls a command called **"Inspection"**. It is only used to check the girls to see if they are in heat with a paper towel. You can figure out the rest from here.

Hug! This is a great command for Shilohs since they love to be close to their owners. Sherri can't have the dogs jump on her because of her balance issues. So I decided to teach Rani and Hera to get hugs sideways. So what I do is, put my arm out with my fist closed and elbow close to my ribs and say **Hug** or **who wants a hug** and they know to jump up and put their front paws on my open arm. Then I pull their head closer to my chest and give them a hug and rub their chest. Rani and Hera are now doing this from a sitting position between my legs and standing up and putting their paws on my two hands connected in front of me to get a hug from behind. ☺

Training can be interesting, fun and challenging. The only advice to give here is to be consistent, give verbal or treat rewards when they do what you ask and never stop training! Your dog will want to please you and the more you teach your pup, the more rewarding it is for both of you.

Potty is a command

What went in now comes out. You have a leash and a collar and now you need to walk your dog to get them the exercise they need and go potty outside in a designated area. Yes, that means you pick the spot you want the dog to go in and get them used to that area. Make sure you clean it up regularly or they will stop using that spot.

We've taught our girls to potty when we want them to. It's a command you can repeat over and over and they will under-stand what to do. Just reward them when they go when they are puppies like they just ran the marathon and won! Yes, make a big deal out of it and reward them when they go potty when and where they are supposed to. This way you shouldn't have any accidents in your house.

Now even as adults when we go on long trips and have to stop so the girls can potty. It is quick and easy to potty all of the girls. We use the potty command and the girls go in no time, rather than taking their time looking for the perfect spot for a half an hour.

How often to go potty?

Puppies do not have a large bladder so they will be going to potty more frequently until they get older. Most puppies already come to you paper trained, so you just need to pick a spot for them to go until you determine what their schedule is for when they need to go potty outdoors.

Make a note when they first start and then take them out every hour and gradually increase the time as they get a couple weeks older. Eventually, you will be able to go four to six hours in between potty times. Of course, there are always those dogs that have weak bladders and just can't hold it. ☺

Potty training a dog is very similar to potty training a child. It takes time and a lot of patience and when they are ready, they are ready. The sooner you introduce paper training, the easier the transition to outdoors.

Once your puppy is well into paper training, one thing that works pretty well (at least for us), is when you know you are going out for an hour or two, don't put down any papers and when you return let your puppy out for potty and praise them for holding it. You will know when to start this routine - typically when the paper is dry when you have left and returned home. You can gradually (each week) increase the time and eventually not having papers on the floor and having your puppy completely housebroken / potty trained. Remember to praise your puppy each and every time they potty outdoors!! This is key to their learning and success.

From the first day, we got Mali I knew she was going to be my service dog and at eleven weeks old I brought her home. When she put her first paw on the ground I was ready to teach her the first thing. Potty Potty. Yes that was it, potty potty. I had already picked the spot where I wanted her to go and she was going to learn to potty on command. At the time, we did not have a fenced in yard and she would have to be taken out on a leash to go, and as a service dog, she would have to know how to go potty on command so she might as well start learning now.

It took Mali less than a day to figure out potty potty, and before the end of the week when she wanted to go out to go potty she would go and get her leash and bring it to me so I could take her out. I know there are two ways of looking at that. Wow, smart dog! She learned to get her leash because she had to go potty in less than a week and she is so young, or Wow, smart dog, she trained her human in less than a week to take her out when she had to go potty! Shilohs!

CHAPTER **4**

What to know about your Shiloh

Do dogs have feelings?

Dogs do have feelings regardless of breed and size, but not like humans.

I believed that too until I met my first Shiloh Shepherd™. These dogs are almost human like in their intelligence and understanding of their people. It often seems as if they have human like feelings as well. In many cases, some of the adult dogs are sure they knew what is best for their owners, better than their owners know what is best for them, and will attempt to make it known to them.

I tend to push myself far more than I should and stay on my feet a lot longer than I should. I really hate being in my wheel chair and since I can walk some, I walk as much as I can. When I over do it I pay for that time by many days of pain after. Because I am always in pain, I tend to ignore pain and just keep pushing getting as much done as I can. It just so happened one day I had a lot of work to do on my feet after a weekend of being on my feet at a dog show.

Mali followed me back and forth in the room vocalizing her distress but I was ignoring her as much as I was ignoring the pain. I just wanted everything finished so I could relax later that night knowing everything was done. Finally, Mali had enough! She took hold of my right arm, she had never done that before and it surprised me. I looked at her but did not pull back, bare skin and sharp teeth do not go good together. Mali led me over to the couch, and with her one hundred pounds, she pushed me onto it. This was a light bulb moment for me as I sat there and looked at her big brown eyes. I needed to sit and she had made it very clear.

Shiloh Temperaments - Soft, Medium, Hard

Since we are on the topic of feelings, it is important you understand that your Shiloh will be one of three types of dog. Soft (please don't yell at me, I didn't do it), Medium (okay, I heard you, but it really wasn't me) and Hard (just talk to the paw why don't you). There are obviously variations to this like a Medium/Soft, etc. Where in some cases you know your dog is a Medium, but he/she tends to think they are in trouble when you're correcting another pack member.

Since there are a range of temperaments, you cannot treat them the same or train them identically the same. Your hard temperament dog may need a bit more convincing than your medium or soft dog. This might mean using a pinch collar instead of a flat or training collar. Shilohs are like human children, sensitive to the tone of your voice, body language and how you are feeling that day. They will tune in on everything. They learn by watching; even things you do not want them to learn. You might think it is so cute when your twelve week old puppy is barking and chasing your vacuum cleaner around while you are cleaning, but how funny will it be when your hundred and twenty pound puppy is doing it. You might think it is amazing when your puppy learns to get an ice cube out of the ice cube dispenser, but how funny will it be when you get up in the morning to a flood in the kitchen because your puppy emptied the ice cube dispenser last night. Do not show your puppy, or encourage your puppy to do anything you do not want it to do later. You have to really think as if your puppy were a human child.

Now I know this goes without saying, but I will state the obvious. Regardless of what your puppy does, remodels your yard, or manages to get to Thanksgiving dinner before you do, you should never ever strike your dog or hurt your dog in any way, shape or form.

Aren't all dogs the same?

You have already read in this book about different temperaments, with these different temperaments come different needs. Some puppies need a more active family and some a family that likes to play at home more. To ensure the right family and puppy find each other it is up to you to be honest when you put in your application with the breeder of your choice.

Are you ready for a dog?

- First and foremost are you ready to get a dog?
- Do you know what's involved with taking care of one, feeding them and ensuring they have proper exercise, food, kibble or raw?
- Have your looked into different veterinarians in your area yet?
- Did you know rubber toys made in China can cause cancer to dogs?
- Do you know what bloat is?
- What about hip dysplasia?
- Have you found a reputable breeder?
- What makes a reputable breeder?
- What kind of collar will you use?

These are just a few of the questions to think about before getting a puppy.

Dogs need exercise

Will your dog require a lot of exercise or is it a couch potato? Are you a couch potato thinking you can handle a very active Shiloh Shepherd™? Don't even consider it if you are!! All dogs (and humans), should exercise or walk regularly. The size of the dog doesn't matter. It is the healthiest thing to do. The real question is how much they need on a daily basis. This comes with their LER (Litter Evaluation Report) and Temperament testing to determine their activity level and if they are a good fit for you. Your breeder will also tell you what their energy level is like.

Collar and Leash

First, you need a collar (flat one to start with) and then you need a 6-foot long leash. One strong enough that will last you, so don't skimp and get a $2 leash and expect it to last long or be strong enough to hold your 100+ pound Shiloh when he/she grows up! We use leather leashes because if the dog suddenly jerks the leash, it will not burn your hand. The leash does not need to be heavy to hold a large dog, just solidly made. ☺

Feeding your dog

You need a bowl for water, a bowl for food (start with large bowls; it'll save you money in the long run). Then based upon your breeder's recommendation, feed your dog as directed/required. Do **NOT** buy the cheap kibble as it is a) not healthy for Shiloh's and b) will not help your Shiloh grow at the rate they normally do. You can expect your Shiloh to put on 3-5 pounds a week at first, which is why they require a high protein diet.

Our girls have been raw fed since we got them. We raw feed all three and it is perfectly safe to do as long as you do it right. They need a high protein diet and beef organs and chicken is good for them. Your breeder will give you food when you first get your puppy and start you on the path to feeding it correctly.

Do all dogs like the same food?

Each puppy may have different appetites and tastes for foods. If you are planning to feed raw foods (chicken and beef), you must follow the guidelines set forth in your contract on what to feed, and on what schedule. When you are unsure when you can change/add something to your puppy's diet, check with your breeder. Puppies do best when fed on a regular schedule while they are growing.

The breeder will tell you the puppies feeding schedule they are on. If you are unable to match the one they are on, it is best to set one up as quickly as possible. As your puppy gets older, it will most likely change its mind when it wants to eat, this is normal. Some puppies are very finicky eaters. Stick to high protein low fat diets. When you bring home a puppy at 8 weeks of age it should be offered food four times a day. Leave the food down for twenty minutes. What it does not consume after twenty minutes pick up and refrigerate for the next meal. As your pup gets a little older you can remove one meal offering three meals a day and can gradually as they get older, offer only two meals a day. Our girls are two years old now and they only want to eat once a day and at night. We have tried offering them a small morning meal and only once in a while will they eat it. Sometimes they will eat a snack during the day, but their main meal is at night. It is best with a large breed of dog to have them eat smaller meals rather than have just one large meal all at one time.

Your new puppy will start out by eating puppy-mash. This is basically, kibble from your breeder which the puppy had been on and is used to, to which you add about a tablespoon non-fat yogurt, vitamins and some raw ground turkey (for the protein). You need to start with some large breed puppy kibble, it is important you use the same brand as the breeder gave you. This will help prevent diarrhea because of a change in diet. You can usually count on some diarrhea because of the stress. You need to keep an eye on it especially when you start changing the food they eat. To help minimize diarrhea, add about a tablespoon pure pumpkin to the pups food as well. Pumpkin is seasonal, so it may be difficult to find it year round. When it is in season, stock up on it for when it is unavailable. We also grow our own pumpkins organically then use a crock pot and slow cook it just enough so we can freeze it. Then we have pumpkin for anytime we need it.

The yogurt helps the puppies digest all the foods. Just a tablespoon is fine with the low-fat plain Yogurt. You can also get probiotics at your local health food stores and add this to your puppy's food. This too, helps you pup digest his food and prevent loose stool.

When you want to introduce a new kibble, it is best to mix it 50/50 with the old kibble so the puppy's digestive system can handle it better. Some puppies with irritable stomachs might need you to go 1/4-3/4 so you may need to experiment to get it right.

Taking your dog out to go potty

Okay, enough about food. You have a leash and a collar and now you need to walk your dog to get them the exercise they need and go potty outside in a designated area. Yes, that means you pick the spot you want the dog to go in and get them used to that area. Make sure you clean it up regularly or they'll stop using that spot.

There WILL be accidents

If you have a puppy, it is most likely still used to paper training, so have plenty of paper ready before you bring him/her in the house. Do not punish your dog or get upset with him/her or rub their noses in the mistake. This does not work and only adds stress to you and your dog. Instead, bring the dog outside on a regular basis (every 2 hours when they are young) until you see they can hold it longer. There are many books on this subject for potty training, so I won't get into more details about this. Just get into a regular routine and make going potty a positive experience!

Pick a spot where you want your dog to be in your home and get them used to being there. They may whimper and whine when you leave the room, but the best you can do is say **"NO"** nicely and walk away. Eventually, and it may take days or even weeks, your dog will understand that spot is his/her area.

CHAPTER 5

Dogs with attitudes

Behavioral Corrections

Shilohs are very much like children as puppies and even into adulthood. When you are trying to train a young puppy not to do something, at first, try redirecting it with something else. For example, when it is trying to use your arm as a chew toy you say, "No bite!" Then stick a plush chew toy in its mouth instead and let it know it is a good puppy. If it is going after something in your home, you do not want to use redirection the same way.

Let's say the Pup got a hold of one of your shoes, you have two options for commands here. You can use "Leave it" or "Not yours". We have taught both to our dogs knowing they will fig-ure out if something is not theirs, they need to learn what they can touch and what they cannot touch in the house. We use leave it when we want them to leave something behind, such as when we want them to leave a muddy toy outside.

The pup has your shoe and has begun to gnaw on it, move close to the pup, say your praise in a firm voice and as you take the shoe away, offer a substitute toy just as you would with a human child.

When you pup is older and you are beginning leash training, there is something called the puppy walk. At this time, you should invest in a good six-foot leather leash. Let your puppy explore the world around him but keep the pup on the left side of you. This will help to teach it later this is the side it will be walking on when it is time to teach the pup to heel.

If your pup should pull you too much while walking, turn around and go the other way. Shilohs are very smart it will not take long for your puppy to figure out if it pulls you, it will not get to go where it wants.

As your pup matures, you may decide you want a training collar. There is a right way and a wrong way to use a training collar. Many people purchase them and use them incorrectly or purchase the wrong size collar for their dog.

The collar should have no more than three inches in length left after it is on the dog. A good collar to buy is a German made collar as they make a great zinging sound when you snap back on them. After all, the idea is not to choke your dog but to get its attention with the sound so close to their ear. It is this sound and the slight pressure that gets the response you want.

If your dog is pulling on the leash, snap the leash back and say **NO.** Each time he pulls, you repeat the correction.

The 'singing sound' can be achieved by quickly pulling up/back on the leash when it is loose to get the dogs attention.

The training collar should be removed when you are not training your dog.

Pull swiftly, but not forcefully

Some of our boys as adolescents and occasionally a girl will need a different collar called a training pinch collar. The first time we looked at this type of collar Mali was only seven months old. I saw the teeth and thought oh no. not on my baby! Those teeth looked like they would tear her neck to shreds. Yes, they could, but you don't pull so hard as to make the dogs head or body spin around - the teeth are like the teeth of an alpha dog. I am her alpha and she needed to understand that I mean to be her alpha all the time not just when she wanted to listen to me. After many masterful escapes I broke down and put a pinch collar on Mali for training and I have to say it did wonders in her training.

If the choker collar no longer works after months or negative behavior and nothing else seems to be working, move up to the pinch collar. The same principal applies here with the exception that there is no singing the pinching collar but the dog **WILL** listen this time.

Teach your dog manners when eating

This may sound funny as were talking about dogs, but the truth is, you don't want your dog to be eating fast and furious or not allow you to take food away from him. Dogs should eat at a steady pace and even break before finishing. Whatever they don't finish in 20 minutes, you can pick up and put away for later.

By controlling how fast they eat, when they eat, and how they eat you can eliminate any food aggression right from day one. You as the alpha should be controlling what your pack can eat and when. This is normal pack behavior where the alpha gets first pick and then everyone else gets what is left.

Eating fast can also contribute to bloat scenarios which you also want to avoid. Bloat can kill your dog in as little as 30 minutes! I highly recommend you do more reading on this subject and be aware of how it comes and treatment options.

Aggression or Possessiveness

When your dog is a puppy, you start teaching it not to be aggressive or possessive of its food or toys and you do this with play. You give your puppy toys and you take them away, but you always return them. When you play tug with your puppy you make sure your puppy wins more than 3/4 of the time as this builds your puppy's confidence and lets it know you will not always take the toy away. However, when playtime is over, it is over. You let the pup know enough is enough and you end the game. If the pup does not wish to stop playing, take hold of him by the scruff of his neck with your hand, not hard but hard enough so he knows it, and in a firm but not yelling voice say, NO. Then stand and turn away avoiding eye contact, or leave the room. Most pups understand right away and do not need a second correction.

Shiloh Shepherds™ are huge dogs as you know by now and having an aggressive or possessive dog would be detrimental to your health and possibly to your pocketbook. Most of our dogs are good-natured, but any dog not socialized and left to fend for itself will not know proper etiquette. So as Ma Shiloh says, "socialize-socialize-socialize!"

As your dog grows older, it is a good idea to not allow any type of aggressive behavior of any kind. I have heard some people say my dog is only aggressive in their den. I personally do not find that acceptable behavior for any dog except a mother with pups. Think about when you have company and your dog is in its crate and your company puts their hand on the crate. What about, you bring your dog to a dog show, and you bring their crate along or an x-pen and the dog then is in the public protecting their den. This is not a safe scenario. Either way someone could get hurt. All it takes is a little time and effort to make sure, this does not happen with your dog when it is a puppy, and through adolescence.

Now no laughing, one way Steve found very successful with helping a puppy understandingnon-food aggression was to pretend he was eating with them. Yes, that means he was down on his hands and knees pretending to eat their food. I am here to tell you it worked! All of our girls will let anyone eat their food. Another option is to feed them small amounts from your hand before giving them their dish as well as, to remove the dish and then return it soon after. Same principal applies to toys.

Biting and nipping

Yelp and walk away: Since puppies are very social animals, refusing to play with them abruptly in play can be an effective training technique. As soon as your puppy starts to bite or nip, give a loud, yelping squeal much like another puppy would make if it were hurt. Then get up and turn your back on the puppy. After a minute or so, get a toy and return to puppy. Encourage the puppy to play with the toy. If he goes for you with a nip, repeat the high pitch yelping and walking away again. This had and affect on my soft girls.

However, on Mali, she thought I was encouraging her to play more. Mali was a super shark puppy and squealing seemed to just encourage her to come for me with gusto. With her we had to use a different technique completely. Every time she tried to bite or nip we redirected her, saying, "No Bite" and at the same time putting something in her mouth appropriate for her to bite; such as a chew toy or a stuffed toy. We also went right into beginning obedience and started her mind on other things besides biting and nipping. The beginning obedience seemed to help just as much as redirection.

We worked Mali's mind with obedience and she forgot about nipping using high valued treats. A high valued treat is something like cooked meats or something healthy. We used cooked chicken cut up into small pieces. We put the pieces into a plastic bag and into a small training pouch. One of the first things we taught Mali was the command WATCH. This command became very valuable later when I needed to get her attention no matter what she was doing.

To keep her "sharkness" down we would take her for long walks every day. We took breaks during our walks so she could rest but we were out for hours at a time. I know most people do not have the luxury of spending hours every day with their dogs, but in training a service dog, Mali needed to be out in the community as much as possible. A tired puppy was a good thing when it came to her "sharkness".

Serious behavioral corrections
(For extreme cases only - talk with your breeder first)

Many Shilohs are very soft; sometimes you will find a medium temperament. Occasionally, you will find a Shiloh Ma calls Medium with ADDITUDE. These young adult dogs have a little more attitude than others and are a little stronger willed. Don't get me wrong, they are just as smart, just as willing to please, just sometimes they might give you a "talk to the paw" when you want them to do a "recall" during training, because a butterfly caught their eye when you want them to come. By the time they are an adolescent, butterflies should be ignorable, so should most other things when you want them to come. This is just one example of a medium with attitude.

There may be times you have to put your dog in a down-stay (on their side) which is a sign of submission. This method is only for more serious behavior corrections so they learn NOT to repeat this behavior.

You can put your dog down by grabbing the side of their neck and collar and twisting and pulling towards you gently and downward until they are on their side. If you are unsure how to do this, get a professional trainer, or your breeder to demonstrate and show you the proper method to correcting your dog in these situations.

You just need to get them down quickly and gently without injuring them. The idea here is to correct their behavior in a positive manner, not make it traumatic, or injure your pet (or you) in the process.

Another time you may need to use a more serious correction is with an adolescent male. Some males when the testosterone starts to flow begin to exhibit "big dog in little dog syndrome". It is true our dogs are large, but their bodies are no anywhere fully gown and their minds at a year or 18 months are not. They are fully capable of procreating at this age and willing to tell and sometimes willing to tell any male they come into contact with just that.

This is a form of aggression you should put a stop to the second you hear the first rumble or see the lip move. A firm NO, and backwards snap of your leash. If that does not work, grab your young boy by the scruff of his neck on either side of his face and lift him off his feet and bring him to your eye level. Repeat firmly, NO! When you put him down again make sure he is not facing the other dog.

If he turns back to the other dog and starts again or goes after another dog right after then it is time to move to another step. This is time for you to move swiftly you will be taking a hold of your dog similar to the paragraph above. Think of your hand as the mouth of dog, take hold of your dog around the scruff of his neck and twist, getting a good hold. With your other hand, you will need to guide the other part of his body down. Now using your weight you will have to pull him towards you to the ground. Move swiftly so your dog does not expect this and as you do loudly say NO!

Once the dog is down, do not let him up. He may struggle, whimper, whine, but do not let him up. He is not only in a submissive position before you, but moments ago the male he was just showing dominance to and now this is a terrible position to be in. At no time, let any other dog near him! Once your dog gives in and relaxes (usually a momentary sigh), you can let him up and continue on with what you were doing. Do not hold anything against him once he is on his feet. The correction was made and now it is time to move on.

Do not body slam your dog down

You just need to get them down quickly and gently without injuring them. The idea here is to correct their behavior in a positive manner, not make it traumatic or injure your pet (or you) in the process.

CHAPTER **6**

Working with your dog

Leaving your home

When it is time to leave the house to go for a walk, out for a car ride, go potty or any other reason, make sure YOU are the first one to leave the house and the dog follows behind you. This sets the stage for you to be the alpha and the dog the follower.

Use the **WAIT** command when you get to the door. We like **WAIT** as it implies a momentary pause. Make sure you have the leash on your dog before getting to the door and have him sitting or waiting in a somewhat calm state. Wait as long as needed until the dog is calm and does not bolt out the door and drag you behind. *You* need to control the dog, not the reverse.

When you are walking, keep the dog to your <u>left</u> side if you show, <u>right</u> side if not. There is a difference and we will talk about that shortly. Your six foot leash is the max the dog should have and as long as the dog isn't pulling you, it's okay if they are at the end of it.

Healing state of mind

Ideally, you want the dog to your side in a **HEAL** state of mind. When they start pulling, you can say **NO PULL** and quickly pull on the leash and make the collar sing. Yes, that was two commands and they will learn not to pull (as hard). You won't break it completely, but just try to keep the leash loose and not tense.

You can also use **HEAL** as a command to alert the dog to walk next to you and not in front of you. This is very useful when you are meeting on coming dogs or humans and need to have the dog closer to you for corrections and/or meet and greet situations. Simply roll up the leash in your hand, but still keep it loose to the dog. It's important that you don't send a signal to the dog to be on alert because you are pulling on the leash.

When you have one dog, this is easier to do. If you have multiple dogs, having them in front or on both sides is equally acceptable. Make sure to train them to be on one side before moving to the other. They are creatures of habit, so don't confuse them.

As you can see below, our girls are in front and to the right.

Stay Calm, Cool and Collected

Try not to exhibit any nervousness or fear when meeting other owners and their dogs as your dog will immediately pick up this fear down the leash. It is important to stay calm, cool and collected while you walk and teach your dog good social skills.

If you encounter another dog, allow your dog to be smelled and to smell - nose to butt, then nose to nose. That's how they get to know one another. Assuming the dog you just met is friendly (and their owner is as well), this is a good time for the meet and greet. Talk to the owner and shake their hand even if it is the first time. This greeting tells your dog that he/she is safe and there is nothing to worry about.

Walking your dog

Your dog(s) will want to use their senses a lot when out for a walk. It's important they have this opportunity to smell and see their surroundings during their walk, so they learn how to work on a leash, how to walk in a pack, how to greet other dogs and their owners and get the right socializing.

Expect to take your dog out at least once a day to socialize with people and other dogs. Taking your dogs to a pet store, sitting outside of a mall, grocery store, or department store and allowing people to come by and greet you and your dog helps greatly with people socializing. Dog parks and walking parks help the dog socialize with other dogs.

Depending on the energy level of your dog, you may need

to walk/run your dog daily to get all that energy out of them. Penned up energy is a time bomb waiting to explode; without sufficient exercise, your dog can become aggressive or chew on things you don't want them too.

After running for about 20 minutes, our girls pose for a picture.

Be prepared for your walk

Once you have your dog sufficiently worn out (a tired dog is a happy dog), they will be easier to train as well. Make sure however, you provide your dog with cold water during those long walks or hot days!

Be aware of hot pavements and asphalt. The pads on their paws can burn very easily and they may not alert you to how serious it is, until it is too late. Test the pavement with your hand and leave it there for about 15 seconds. If it gets too hot for your hand, it's generally too hot for their paws!

There are booties you can buy for locations where it is near impossible to walk without having something on their paws. Alternatively, take them for a walk in the early morning or later in the evening when the surface of the pavement is not as hot.

Handling Summary

As you can see, there is a lot to handling your dog. There are other books you can find on each topic I've listed and they will get into greater detail as well. Ideally, treat your dog as if you have a child and want to teach your child right from wrong with positive reinforcement.

In the beginning, it is always useful to have a treat bag on you so you can reward them when they are doing well. This is the best time to treat them, as they will associate good behavior with treats they like to eat. Don't over do it either, you don't want your dog to get fat from too many positive behaviors!

Rewards versus Treat

Another good reward for your dog is telling him/her when they are good. "Good girl Mali, good girl!" You don't need to give them a treat when you are rewarding them with words or a pat on their head or body. They are perfectly happy with that too! To build confidence reward them and lift and rub gently under their chin and praise them.

My dog does not like treats

This is perfectly normal and not uncommon. Not all dogs are treat motivated so you need to come up with a different motivation and reward for them. This could just be more pats on their head, a special toy they know and love, or something else they really enjoy. It is up to you to monitor what gets your dog motivated and excited to use in your training.

CHAPTER 7

Socializing and Fear Periods

Socializing begins at four weeks of age and while some say it ends at 16 weeks, it really never ends. The first 16 weeks of a puppy's life is the primary socializing period when the dog is introduced to other dogs, species, people, objects, sights and sounds. The real socializing begins on a regular basis to reinforce what they have learned earlier and to build up their confidence level. Socializing helps your dog to become confident in their life. It also helps them to not become aggressive or afraid of other dogs, animals, people or even objects and noises.

Starting at four weeks and ending with 16 weeks, your puppy will go through all sorts of phases including "fear periods." During the fear periods, it is important that more praises are provided to help instill the confidence they may already have or may still need.

Puppy Development

Day 1 - 3 weeks

- From day 1 to day 14, the puppy cannot see or hear. They rely solely on the mothers nurturing skills or human help to make sure they eat and gain wait properly - about 1-3 ounces per day is good. The puppy cannot regulate their body temperature during this time, so a heat lamp and thermometer may be required to make sure the temperature in the whelping box stays between 74-80 degrees.

- Day 15 to 3 weeks, the puppies may move around more and not need the heat lamp. Keep an eye on the puppies during this time as you may need to continue it longer for one or more of them. Taking their temperature (rectally) will help determine when to remove the heat.

Socialization and Personality Development

4 weeks - 16 weeks

- During this period, puppies need opportunities to meet other dogs and people.

- From 3 to 5 weeks puppies are becoming aware of their surroundings, companions (dogs and people), and relationships. They are also learning how to play.

- From 4 to 6 weeks puppies are most influenced by their littermates and are learning about being a dog and how to play.

- From 4 to 12 weeks puppies are most influenced by their littermates and people. They are also learning to play, including social skills, inhibited bite, social structure/ ranking and physical coordination.

- From 5 to 7 weeks they are developing curiosity and exploring new experiences. Your puppy needs positive "people" experiences during this time.

- From 7 to 9 weeks puppies are refining physical skills / coordination (including house training) and full use of senses.

- From 8 to 10 weeks they experience real fear -- puppies can be alarmed by normal objects and experiences and need positive training.

- From 9 to 12 weeks they are refining reactions, social skills (appropriate interactions) with littermates and are exploring the environment, spaces and objects. They are beginning to focus on people. This is a good time to begin more basic training.

- After 12 weeks, most influenced by "littermates" (playmates now include those of other species).

- After 12 weeks, beginning to see and use ranking (dominant and submissive) within the pack, including with humans.

- Teething (and associated chewing) starts early on about 4 weeks and continues until their adult teeth come in around 6 months.

- At four months (16 weeks) they experience another fear stage.

The previous page identifies typical periods in the dog's development where we can accurately mold and shape the dogs behavior for the rest of their lives. Improper or inadequate socializing can have a negative impact on your dog's ability to meet other dogs, animals and even humans in a positive manner. Socializing does not just end in the first few months or even the first year of their life. You must continue with positive socialization throughout the dog's life so there are no unexpected or unwanted accidents. After all, would you stop socializing your one year old baby boy or girl, or give your child the socializing they need to be a positive influence in society?

Please refer to the link in Chapter 14 on Proper Puppy Socializing for Shiloh Shepherds™.

CHAPTER 8

Can I show my Shiloh?

Showing

Showing your dog can be the most fun and exhilarating experience you will ever do with your dog. Not only does the dog shine and show off what they can do, but you also get to exercise and strut your stuff too! This is a win-win experience and something that you will want to continue for a long time.

Benefits of Showing

What are the benefits of showing? Your dog gets recognized by other breeders, judges and the audience watching. You can hopefully champion the dog and if you breed, it goes a long way to show the potential of the puppies they have. To champion a dog, one needs to win the required number of points determined by your breed club which then identifies your dog as a champion (winner) of all dogs in your club. Each club can have many champions and Grand Victors (highest class).

As you can see from the photo above, the ring can be very busy and challenging -- especially for those juniors who are showing for the first time. It is a great event for kids and they get to be part of the fun and excitement too.

What do I wear?

You should wear comfortable sneakers or shoes as well as clothing that fits you well.Dress nicely and do not wear torn, dirty or worn clothing. Dress like you are giving a performance and all the eyes are on you and your dog - as they will be when you are in the ring. Dress nice, look good and feel good while you show your dog!

What does it cost to Show?

It can get expensive to show your dog but there are clear benefits for doing this in the end. Each showing event can cost you $20 and up per show and some events have 1-5 shows in a weekend.

So for one dog it is relatively inexpensive, but if you have 2, 3 or more, it can get expensive. You will also have to weigh in the cost of traveling to the event, the hotel and the event itself.

It is very easy to drop about $500 in a weekend just for one Dog Show. Make sure this is what you want and are able to afford.

There are some tips and techniques to showing your dog and I will get into that part shortly. But first, let's talk about what the judge is looking for when you have your dog in the ring.

What does a Judge look for?

Pay close attention to what the judge wants you to do. Follow others (if someone is in front of you), or simply repeat back to the judge (if you are unsure) what they want you to do. Once you get the hang of it, it will become easy. Some judges are all business and no play! This means they just want to judge your dog and are less interested in having idle conversations with you, in training you, or spending any extra time with you or your dog.

As I've stated earlier, watch others and what the judge is doing and saying. This will go a long way before you get in the ring.

Watch the Judge

Each judge has their own personal prefer-ence about what they like to see. This in-cludes movement, body mass, energy level, bone structure, height, temperament, coat and

many other aspects which they look at while you show your dog.

Judges also critique you about how you show your dog and handle them in the ring. How you run with the dog is equally important as the dog running themselves. Sorry, you don't get trophies or ribbons when your dog does. It's all about the dog, not you -you are simply there for the ride! ☺

Physical Requirements

If you really enjoy showing dogs and like the excitement of it all, that's great! We need more people like you dedicated to showing off what our dogs can do. Just make sure you are physically able to do what it takes to be in the ring. This is not only a **financial** challenge, but **physical** and **mental** challenge to both you and your dog.

The more you practice the better you do and the better you appear in the ring. You need to have the endurance to potentially run a couple miles in one show depending on how well your dog does.

Your running around the ring should compliment your dog. You don't want the dog pulling you or you pulling the dog. You should both be running at the same speed and look good together. This is what makes a winning team! Learn what your dog's pace is and what shows off her stride the best. You will need to practice running at different speeds until you get the right one. ☺

What can my dog win?

Here are some titles to illustrate the number of times you may be running for a judge. Each win results in moving to the next category to show in.

- Winners Bitch/Dog - first win against all the dogs in the ring
- Best of Winners Bitch/Dog - second level win against all dogs in the ring
- Best of Opposite - third level, but you won against the opposite sex (male or female) in the ring
- Best of Breed - forth level win where your bitch/dog was the best of all the other dogs of your breed that day
- Best in Show - final level where your dog is recognized as the best of all dogs shown that day

How much running is there really?

For each showing event, you can count on a minimum of two times running around the ring. That's about 10 times around per show and some events have two shows a day for two days. That's a lot of running!! J

Bring plenty of water and be hydrated before and after you show. Same for your dog as he/she can easily overheat and completely shut down (not want to show), and then you are just wasting your time and money.

CHAPTER **9**

Show Preparation and Tips

Practice before showing

As stated earlier, make sure that before you go in the ring, you watch the judge and learn what he/she is looking for and what comments they are making about other dogs. This will help you show off your dogs attributes even more. Practice outside the ring somewhere and get your dog ready for the event. Don't wear him/her out, just get them (and you) prepared for what is coming.

Grooming

Make sure you have groomed/brushed out your dog prior to all shows. The judge does not want to get a hand full of dog hair when they are inspecting your dog's coat, legs, and belly. Take the time to make your dog not only looks good running around the ring, but also being in the ring as well.

Keep your distance

One of the most important parts to showing your dog is to KEEP YOUR DISTANCE from the dog in front of you. If you know your dog runs fast, this doesn't mean the one in front will. Give the person in front of you enough distance to run, so you can let your dog show the best.

Don't lag too far behind either or you'll lose points that way too. Don't worry too much about this as the judge will notice how well your dog runs (and you), but keeping about 6-10 feet of space between you and the dog in front of you provides your dog with breathing room and room to move around if needed.

It is not uncommon for the judge to ask you to move in front or behind someone else so they can see the full potential of your dog.

Show Leash versus Walking Leash

Make sure you have the right type of leash in your hand and on the dog. This is not the normal walking leash, it's a leash specifically designed for showing off your dog. When you run with your dog, the leash (all of it) stays in the left hand only and loose enough to not choke your dog, but all the way up the neck to direct them around the ring. This is required - you do not use a normal leash or collar when showing your dogs.

When you have your show leash on, this is all that the dog wears. There are no other collars present, it's all about showing and this is what you both focus on.

Show leashes are inexpensive. You want one that is a light-weight chain that goes around the neck, and that will stay in place while you run.

Do not choke your dog

It is very easy to put the leash on incorrectly and harm your dog in the ring. Do not have it too tight as the dog cannot breathe. Adjust it as necessary every time you prepare to go around the ring.

Practice running around a circle to the left

This is a difficult one for beginners and beginner dogs. You need to make sure you don't trip over your dog going around the ring. One thing to practice with your dog, is to have them to go around the ring naturally turning left all the way.

Why do I say this? Your dog will instinctively feel like they are hugging your left knee and almost trip you (and yes this does happen). Practicing and teaching your dog a command like **"SHOW"** or **"LEFT"** to signify they are showing and you expect them to run around in a circle going left all the way is vital to showing successfully. This takes a lot of practice, but has worked great for our girls.

Before you go in the ring

Make sure your dog is not too thirsty and has had a chance to go potty. You do NOT want an accident in the ring. While this happens from time to time, it can almost always be avoided. Make sure you always come with doggy bags just in case you do have an accident in or near the ring. Puppies are known for having accidents, but adult dogs can be disqualified.

What is a Win Sheet?

Each club has win sheets which are used to record how many dogs showed and. what place yours came in at. Depending on how well you do, you earn points towards championship. Check with your club for rules and regulations.

Complete and bring your win sheets for the club you are showing your dogs in. It is most helpful to print out some win sheets and have them ready to be completed and signed by the Chairperson and Judge when you do win. If you don't complete this win sheet, you don't get points towards championship which is the main goal of showing.

Win sheets can be completed ahead of time and filling in the show dates, names, and class entered when you arrive is fine. As your dog progresses, you may want to enter them into multiple classes and shows.

You should mail in your win sheets as soon as you return home (make a copy for your records). They typically need to be mailed within one to two weeks after the show to get the points counted for that show. Make sure you fill in all the details. If it is incomplete, it may not be accepted or counted.

Dog behavior during shows

Pay attention to your dog's behavior. Keep him/her encouraged while preparing for the ring and during the show. Make sure you keep your dog focused on the show and what is expected. This can be best achieved by practicing outside of the ring so your dog gets familiar with this part of their training. All showing is, is another extension of their training and what you expect of them. Make it fun, exciting, and expect them to do more and better each time.

It should be rewarding, so have their favorite treats to keep them actively engaged.

Nice Teeth

The judge will want to see your dog's teeth and bite - practice saying something like **"Nice Teeth"** and then lifting up on both their upper cheeks/gums to expose their teeth. The front teeth view and side views are what the judges will want to look at. They will either ask you to do it, or they will want to, but always wait for them to ask.

Stacking

Stacking is a term used to describe a dog's leg position when showing. This position is required at all shows, and is therefore important to practice.

The dog's left rear leg (from foot to elbow) should be straight up and down.

To get your dog into a stacked position, lift your dogs left rear leg up gently by the elbow and position their leg so it is straight up and down. Move the right leg slightly inwards. This makes a natural pose for the dog and a comfortable stand for them.

The front two paws should be even with each other. If they are not, you can gently lift up each one and let the dog put them down and they will generally align naturally for you. The tail should be straight down and not tucked between the legs.

Incorrect Stacking

Do not reach over your dog to stack and adjust your dog's leg positions. The judge is on the other side and is looking at your dog and won't get the best view if you are leaning over and lifting up a leg. ☺

There are several ways to adjust your dog to get the best exposure and I highly recommend attending classes to see how your club recommends doing it. You can then tailor what you have learned with what other judges may like.

Training never ends

Training does not stop (ever) when you own a dog. This is one of the biggest misconceptions that most people face. Some think that if they have trained their dog to sit, come, down and stay, "What more should I need to do?" People often say, "He's an obedient dog and does what I ask". Our theory is that you treat your dog as a member of your pack and you teach your pack member until the dog is not able to learn something new.

Yes, old dogs CAN learn new tricks. Don't believe every old tale you hear. ☺

Shiloh's are intelligent

Shiloh's on the other hand are very intelligent and want to learn and to please you. Yes, I said that right. They want to please you and they want to learn. Challenge your dogs like you would a human child, and teach new commands, new tricks; involve them in Search and Rescue, Herding opportunities, Service Dog training, and other types of training. Your dog will appreciate it and so will you. You will both see the results and you both earn them!

CHAPTER 10

Medical and Veterinary

How to tell when your dog may be ill

One of the most important parts of being a dog owner is getting to know who your pet is and when they may not be feeling well. They cannot communicate in human terms, so you have to learn to read their body language and know the sign as they present themselves before it is too late. Some symptoms can be life threatening and seeking medical attention immediately may be required.

While your veterinary doctor has all the labs and resources at their finger tips, there are steps you can take to determine when your pet needs medical attention.

- ***Take your dogs temperature*** - this is done rectally and you can use a $5 thermometer that gives you an instant read out in seconds. If the temperature is less than 100 degrees or more than 103 degrees, you want to contact your veterinary hospital and provide them with all the symptoms.

- ***Is your dog behaving differently?*** - More often than not, when your dog's behavior changes this is a sign that something may be wrong. Changes include: restlessness, sleeping excessively, walking and rubbing their butt on the floor, excessive thirst, lack of appetite, vomiting, diarrhea or bad breath (more than normal). These are only a few, so it is up to you to pay attention to when your dog behaves normally to determine an abnormal or atypical behavior they may be showing.

Finding a vet

Location

One of the most important steps to owning "any" pet, not just a Shiloh is to make sure you have a very good Veterinary Doctor you can rely on. If you are searching for the first time (in most cases for a beginner), you want to find a vet within 30 minutes (if you can) of your home. The reason is for emergency situations; if you have an emergency, you want to be close enough to save your pet and not have to drive too far to get help. Alternatively, if there is a Pet Hospital nearby you can take you dog there as well. Just do you homework before an emergency happens and plan where it is you will take your dog when you need urgent care.

Large Breed Dogs

The second thing to look for is a Veterinary Doctor who is familiar and can treat "large breed dogs." Not all vets can or are familiar with large breed dogs and it is important you find someone that is, so you can feel confident your dog is in good hands. The size is not the only thing to consider. Your vet should also be able to handle most, if not all, of the health concerns which may arise. Large dogs have deep chests and are more at risk to have bloat. Not all veterinary hospitals are equipped to handle this serious medical issue.

If your vet has treated other large breed dogs like a Bernese Mountain Dog, Newfoundland, Bullmastiff or Great Dane, they will be familiar with how fast they grow and the proteins they need in order to be healthy.. Large breed dogs require more protein in their diets so that their bones receive enough nutrients to grow properly.

Raw Feeding

Find out how your vet feels about raw feeding your dog. Some vets are totally against it, because they have not done enough research on it and/or they don't believe owners can handle counting calories, proteins, fat, ounces, etc to ensure they have an equally balanced meal. They also are concerned about salmonella and other issues. It is up to you to either provide the details they need to feel comfortable with how you feed your dog or go to another vet.

We raw feed all our girls and puppies. They have been on raw food since they were old enough to eat on their own. We feel (as well as the breed founder) that it is the best source of protein in their diets.

Veterinary Services Available

You dog will require specific testing as they get older if you plan on breeding him/her. Having a vet that can test their hips/elbows is a plus. This test is a Penn HIP (for their hips) and OFA for their elbows, where they take pictures of the hips and elbows (sedated).The purpose of the test is to ensure no genetic faults are present before you breed. We do not want to bring in unhealthy puppies when we can minimize the risk. The cost of this test can range from $300 - $800 depending on the vet and their expertise. Spending more does not mean you are getting better results either, it just means that the vet charges more because they are probably using "human grade anesthesia" which is recommended.

Having a vet who can do blood tests and can process the results in-house is always better, because you don't have to wait for them to send the results out, have them processed, returned and then you get notified days or weeks later. You want results fast so you can deal with anything that comes up more quickly and provide the care you feel is appropriate to your pet.

Obviously, a full service veterinary hospital is better than one which only offers the basic care and treatments for your pets. You may find you need to use several vets for different services and this is okay too. We have actually used six vets over the last few years for a variety of reasons. We have two primary vets we use; one is for everyday treatments and the other is a specialist in breeding and can provide Penn HIP and other types of services.

Shots and Vaccinations

Duramune - When you get a new puppy, he/she should have had some of their shots. Puppies need to get three Duramune shots which protect them from: Distemper, Hepatitis, Adenovirus Type 2, Parainfluenza, Caronavirus and Parvo. Some of the viruses in the vaccine are modified but still alive and some are killed. By taking these viruses into their bodies, dogs become naturally able to fight off the same diseases if they come in contact with them later in life. Humans receive vaccines in a similar way and for the same reasons.

Heartworm protection – This should be administered on a monthly basis and the amount is determined by the puppy's weight. Once they reach 25 pounds, they should be able to take Heartguard which is what we provide to our dogs. Heartguard is a simple, low-cost, effective method of preventing heartworms. A prescription is required to obtain Heartguard because one must be sure that your pet is not already infected with the parasite. Giving preventatives to an animal that already has heartworms may cause serious or possibly fatal side effects.

Rabies Shots – This should be done as soon as possible. In our breed, we typically wait until the dog is about six months old. State and local laws may dictate other requirements, but if you can wait until they are six months old, it is better for your dog. This allows the dog's immune system to grow and be ready for the rabies shot.

Lyme Disease - If you are near woods or in an area where Lyme Disease is prominent, you want to make sure your dog is vaccinated against this disease. Certain ticks found on deer harbor bacterium in their stomachs. Lyme disease is spread by these ticks when they bite the skin, which permits the bacterium to infect the body. Lyme disease is not contagious from an infected person to someone else or from dog to human. Lyme disease can cause abnormalities in the skin, joints, heart, and nervous system.

Health concerns

Bloat (Gastric Dilatation-Volvulus "GDV")

This condition is more likely to occur in large dog breeds. Bloat is a condition in which there is a rapid accumulation of air in the stomach causing abnormal swelling. The real problem begins if a volvulus (or torsion) occurs. This happens when the dilated stomach twists, cutting off contact with the esophagus at one end and the small intestine at the other, trapping the air. The twisted stomach puts pressure on the blood vessels, twisting them in the abdominal cavity and impairing blood flow back to the heart. This then, , decreases blood to the rest of the body, because of a lack of blood left to pump. The dog is in excruciating pain. Soon the stomach begins to die, and without blood flow to the rest of the body the dog's organs begin to fail and the dog looses consciousness; death is imminent.

How do you know if your dog has bloat?

In some dogs it may be an obviously distended stomach, near the last ribs, but in other dogs you cannot see this at all. Either way, if you put your hand there and lightly press on the stomach it will feel hard like the surface of ball or a drum. The dog, being in such pain, will exhibit symptoms such as: appearing restless, circling, and lying down only to repeat this over and over as they just cannot get comfortable. The dog may whimper and whine, but the biggest clue to look for is **non-productive gagging, vomiting, and coughing.**

Although your dog will feel very nauseated, he/she will not be able to bring up much more than drool. They will drool excessively, after all they are unable to swallow with their stomach closed off and they will be unable throw up. The dog may attempt to defecate, but remember with his twisted stomach that end is closed off also. This is part of anxious behavior exhibited along with pacing, air licking and whining you may see.

Other signs to look for in your dog would be a dog that stands in a roached position. This means with his/her back curved up high and its head and butt down. It could stand with its legs spread wide, or even curl into a tight ball. All of these positions are the dogs attempt to find a comfortable position to get away from the pain in their stomach. Some dogs have even been known to eat foreign objects to try to rid themselves of the pain such as bark, twigs, and rocks. Here is one website you can visit to see pictures of a Shiloh Shepherd™ who received treatment for bloat: http://www.dogbreedinfo.com/articles/caninebloatdiary.htm.

What can you do to save the life of your dog?

IF YOU SUSPECT THAT YOUR DOG HAS BLOAT, RUSH IMMEDIATELY TO YOUR VETERINARIAN. SPEED IS IMPORTANT!

The rate of stomach tissue death is quick. The intense pain with Bloat can cause increased heart rhythm, leading to heart failure and shock. Treatment must be within one to two hours. There can be no recovery until the stomach is untwisted and the gas released. For days later you have to wait and see if the dog will survive. Surviving the surgery is just the first step; they now must survive the return of their blood to the organs. In recent years there has been development of a new surgery which can be performed. While they are inside, they can tack your dogs stomach. This surgery is called gastropexy; it tacks your dog's stomach in place so it will not be able to bloat again. This same surgery can be done on a healthy dog so it can never Bloat to begin with.

Prevention of Bloat

Veterinarians will admit not knowing what really prevents Bloat, but they each have their own theories. Bloat is a great debate in the veterinary world. What everyone can agree on, is that it is the second leading cause of death in large and giant breeds after cancer. Deep chested, (rather than wide) narrow and deep abdomens show higher incidence of Bloat. Underweight dogs are at higher risk than overweight dogs, and older dogs more than young. These facts are not causational, meaning that just because your dog has a deep abdomen does not mean he WILL get Bloat, but rather co relational. If your dog has a deep abdomen they are more likely to get Bloat.

Bloat Facts

Great Danes, Dobermans, German Shepherds, are all in the top 12 list of dogs that get Bloat. You can see Shiloh Shepherds™, by being close cousins to the German Shepherds, puts them right up there for risk of the condition.

The experts agree that rapid eating habits and eating only one meal a day contributes to the possibility of Bloat, as opposed to two or more small meals a day. We feed our girls two small meals a day and snacks. There is a huge debate about raised and non-raised food bowls, which I will not get into. I will leave this for you to do your own research on. I will though, talk about the higher incidences of Bloat with dog food. Dry foods containing citric acid, as a preservative, especially if moistened, along with gas producing ingredients such as soybean products, brewer's yeast, alfalfa, and also fat in the first four ingredients, increases the possibility of bloat. For that matter, any dry food containing corn, barley, flour, or any other grain puts the dog at higher risk. Grains, when moist, grow. Grains were not meant to be fed to dogs, so it is best to feed the correct food to the correct species. There is grain free kibble out there if you do not wish to raw feed. A raw fed dog and a grain free dog are less likely to bloat, as they do not have large amounts of gas in their stomachs.

Limit exercise for at least a half an hour before feeding and for an hour after. Why? Dogs who exercise on a full stomach are more likely to have their stomachs twist. Our girls all know after they eat it is time for an hour nap, no excuses. We start this even as puppies. We know puppies cannot Bloat but we start the rituals of our house from the moment they enter our lives. If you kibble feed, you should limit the amount of water your dog has when they eat. They should wait until after their nap, and then only small amount at first. There is still a debate as to if this affects bloat or not but we like to err on the safe side. Dogs that are raw fed drink much less water as raw meat is moist and has higher water content.

Demodectic Mange (Demadex)

Here is a rather nasty disease that spreads very quickly and typically occurs in young puppies, who do not have fully developed immune systems. Demodectic Mange (Demodecosis) is caused by an external parasite that is also present in low numbers on healthy animals, including people. The parasite attacks when the animal is under stress? There are no quick or easy tests to determine a dog's immune status, so it is impossible to predict which pets will get this disease, or how well a pet will heal if it shows symptoms of demadex. There are things you can do to help minimize this risk. Reduce the pets stress level. Do NOT microchip your pet before six months of age. This can lead to stress and cause an outbreak. Provide you dog with Vitamin C to help boost the immune system. Check with your vet on the proper dosage for your pet.

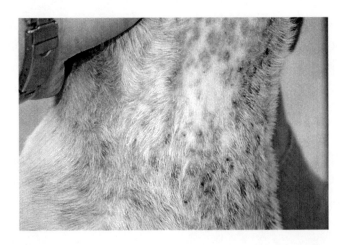

Common Symptoms

Demadex can appear just about anywhere on the pet's body. It can be between their toes which is very painful, on their chest, back, legs and even their head/face. It appears like the fur has fallen off and it can be bumpy and painful to the pet when you touch it. Corrective surgery is available and can cost you $350 and up to treat. The sooner is it is addressed, the less expensive it will be to treat. There are different antibiotics and treatments available. Consult with your veterinary doctor and your breeder to determine the best course of action for your dog.

Roundworms

This is a disease which affects dogs and is caused by the intestinal parasitic roundworm (or Ascaris lumbricoides). Roundworms are often quite large -- up to 10 to 12 centimeters in length (or about 4 inches) -- and can be present in extremely high numbers within an infected animal. When they are found in a dog's body, it can lead to abdominal swelling (distension), colic, gastrointestinal issues, and even intestinal rupture.

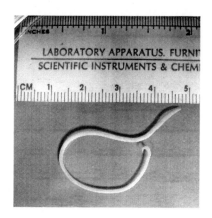

Common Symptoms

Colic, Lethargy, Vomiting, Abdominal swelling, Abnormal feces, Poor nursing (in females), Anorexia, Coughing (caused when the roundworm larvae have migrated into the dog's lungs). Adult dogs can become infected through the ingestion of roundworm eggs, which are found in infected food, water, vomit, or feces. Pups can then contract the parasite during the pregnancy or by drinking the milk from an infected pregnant animal. If one of the newborns in a litter is exposed to roundworms, the entire litter can contract the parasite. One treatment we found very successful is using Panacur. You should read the instructions on how to use it for the weight of your dog. This is one of the best medicines on the market and kills the roundworms after 3 consecutive treatments. Once your dog is old enough, they should be put on a monthly treatment of heartworm medication which typically includes treatment for roundworms.

Parvo

The Canine Parvovirus (CPV) infection is a highly contagious viral illness that affects dogs. The virus manifests itself in two different forms. The more common form is the intestinal form, which is characterized by vomiting, diarrhea, weight loss, and lack of appetite (anorexia). The less common form is the cardiac form, which attacks the heart muscles of very young puppies, often leading to death. The majority of cases are seen in puppies that are between six weeks and six months old. The incidence of canine parvovirus infections has been reduced radically by early vaccination in young puppies. This is a virus you want to avoid at all costs. When you take your puppy to the veterinary hospital, carry your pet and do not put them on the floor or ground until you have at least three shots. Yes, your pet will be heavy to carry, but this precautionary measure is well worth it in the end. Check with your vet to learn about Parvo in your area and to see how prominent it is. If you are in a high Parvo area, you want your dog to have three or four shots before you start taking your puppy for walks in the park.Parvo can be contracted by your dog sniffing an infected dog's feces or carried in from someone's shoes where you may have stepped on an infected area. It is highly contagious and a deadly virus!

Common Symptoms

The major symptoms associated with the intestinal form of a Canine Parvovirus infection include severe, bloody diarrhea, lethargy, anorexia, fever, vomiting, and severe weight loss. The intestinal form of CPV affects the body's ability to absorb nutrients, and an infected animal will quickly become dehydrated and weak from lack of protein and fluid absorption. The wet tissue of the mouth and eyes may become noticeably red and the heart may beat too rapidly. When your veterinarian palpates (examines by touch) your dog's abdominal area, your dog may respond with pain or discomfort. Dogs that have contracted CPV may also have a low body temperature (hypothermia), rather than a fever.

Exocrine Pancreatic Insufficiency (EPI)

EPI refers to failure of the pancreas to normally secrete digestive enzymes. This results in diarrhea and weight loss, often despite the fact that the animal's appetite has increased. While EPI occurs in both dogs and cats, the most common cause is different in each species. EPI in dogs is usually due to a condition called Pancreatic Acinar Atrophy, or PAA, but in cats it is most commonly due to end-stage pancreatitis.

Common Symptoms

Clinical signs associated with Exocrine Pancreatic Insufficiency include weight loss, polyphagia (eating too much), coprophagia (eating their own feces), pica (eating dirt, chalk, paper, etc), diarrhea, increased borborygmus (gurgling, rumbling noise in abdomen), and flatulence (gas). Routine diagnostic tests eliminate some of these as possibilities. Once EPI is suspected, there are specific laboratory tests that can be used for a diagnosis. Blood tests and fecal tests are normal and expected.

CHAPTER 11

Shiloh Short Stories

Z and the Screen Door

Linda and Z (another Shiloh from New York) came to visit to court and mate with Yuki. She was not quite ready yet, so they came to stay for a week. Our pen for the dogs encompasses the door off our back porch. After a couple of hours visiting, Z was put outside with the girls to play but he was not happy to be there without his mom. He tried whining, scratching, yowling. And just about anything to get her attention. We kept the kitchen door open so we could see the dogs on the porch and they could see us while we visited.

Z decided my screen door did not need to have a straight screen any longer, and busted through it. Steve went out with Linda's permission, and reminded him he was not the alpha dog at this house. Then Steve straightened and reinserted the screen back into the door.

The following day, Z had decided the screen did not need to be there at all and went all the way through it. He got himself stuck half way through the door; half on the porch and half on the steps outside. When Steve got to him, the screen could not be saved. I have to admit, biting my tongue was all I could do to not laugh at that huge dog stuck in between my porch and the screen door. I felt bad for Linda as she was obviously beside herself and embarrassed about the damage, but we just said that "dogs do stuff."

That was the beginning of the end of Z's tantrums. When he returned home, Linda had enough of his "little boy" behaviors and took him to see Lisa (the breed founders daughter) for some one-on-one training. Now her boy has grown up, is very well behaved, and shows handsomely in the ring. - Sherri

Filling up at the Gas Station

One day we were out and about with the girls (Mali, Rani and Yuki) and we had to stop to get gas. As a rule, I always put down the back windows so they can watch me fill up the tank and wash the windows. This day was just a little different and out of the normal routine. You see, we stopped behind another vehicle at the pump and a woman got out of her car from the passenger side and proceeded towards us before I could get out of the car.

As the woman came closer she was smiling and clearly excited to see three large heads protruding from my car. She came right up to the window and reached her hands out and started to pet the dogs before asking. Of course our girls have been properly socialized and a hand is free to lick and rub on, so she got tons of loving from all three dogs.

When we asked the woman why she just reached in she said, "I just love dogs and they looked friendly enough." She went along her merry way and I filled up the tank of gas and we left.

Sherri and I said to one another, we were thankful we trained our girls not to be den and car aggressive. We encourage people (usually invited), to pet our girls while they are in the car. We feel it is all part of the socializing they need and should have. In fact, we have gone to great lengths to ensure none of them are aggressive in any way.

You may be wondering, is this a safe thing to do? Absolutely! Our girls are smart, as with any Shiloh, and if we were in any danger, they would have alerted (barked or growled) when someone came near which could have been a threat. They just know that when we say it is okay, then they need to behave accordingly, and they do! - Steve

Escape from the Pen

One early morning, we are in the living room and the girls (Mali, Rani, Yuki and Hera) are all out in the back yard playing. We are watching television and can hear them playing with one another like they do any other day. Then all of a sudden, it gets pretty quiet as we have our backdoor open and can hear them pretty well. A few moments go by and then Rani kicks the door with her front paws (as she does when she wants in) and she barks several times.

Well, this is not quite the normal behavior so Sherri goes to the door to find Rani standing there and the gate (x-pen) is pulled away from the house and the other three girls are no where in site. Rani decided to stay behind and tattle tale on the others. Sherri comes to wake me up (it was a weekend and I try to get some sleep) about 7:45am and says the girls escaped! So I jump up and get dressed and drive down to our neighbor's house since this is where they always go. There are other dogs (in pens) along with some loose chickens and hens they like to chase.

Yuki comes right to Sherri and gets in her car (she was there already) and Mali is still not coming. Evelyn (our neighbor) comes outside and tries to call Mali to her and Mali says, no way I want those chickens first. She chases them right up into the trees. Evelyn then gets a cup of kibble she feeds to her dogs and offers it to Mali. Mali being food motivated as she is say, hmmm, I do not get that at home, let me try some. She does, and then Evelyn reaches out and holds Mali by the collar so I can come get her. Evelyn is an elderly lady and Mali probably weighs more than she does, but with her Service Dog training, she knows not to pull away.

I reach Mali and she is all excited to eat some kibble and then comes with me to the car and we drive back home, still not knowing where Hera is. We had just hoped she returned on her own. We arrive home and sure enough, there she is with that big grin on her face saying....what?? I've been here the whole time, like we didn't know.

That's an adolescent 10 month old for you. At least she came home on her own and went right back in the pen. Needless to say, the x-pen extension to their fenced in area is not working any more as they know how to pull it away from the house. Time to put some chain link fencing in!

Update: we found out that Hera is the one who learned how to pull the x-pen away from the house to escape. They succeeded two more times until we had to lock it against the house!

CHAPTER 12

Shiloh Types and Upgrading

How many types of Shilohs are there?

Now here is a very good question! First, let's clarify what this means. We are talking about the coat types. Shiloh Shepherds™ come in a variety of coat colors in both long (plush) and short hair (smooth). In our breed, a long haired dog is a "Plush" and a short haired dog is a "Smooth."

We also have many color variations and there is a link in Chapter 14 for Shiloh Shepherd™ Coat Colors where you can download a PDF document showing all the different colors in this breed.

Personality / Temperament Differences

Does having a plush or smooth coat dictate what type of personality / temperament that dog will have? No, personalities and temperaments are both genetic and environmentally molded into the dog. For example, if you don't socialize your puppy during the 4-16 week period, it is more than likely to have fear and aggressive tendencies. This is because they were not exposed to all the different social elements they should have been exposed to, when they were learning and developing.

Smooth versus Plush coats & Shedding

Many people want to know which type of dog will shed more than the other. Well, for Shilohs, the Smooth Coat dog will appear to shed more and the Plush less. However, both coat types will blow (shed) their coats about twice a year. One thing that has helped us is to use a Furminator brush. This gets right to the undercoat and removes all of that excess fur. Brushing at least once a week also helps keep it under control.

How many dogs should I get?

This is up to you and what you can handle. Keeping in mind the dogs' personality, energy level, and what you can properly support your new family member with. Having one dog may be great and easy on you for their exercise, but dog boredom can become an issue. This is when your dog becomes so bored, they start doing things in your home you do not want them to. Their behavior could become destructive (chewing furniture and other incidentals). Having a second dog helps them to be pack oriented and they have someone to play with. This does not mean they both won't chew your furniture, but it may minimize the risk. Sometimes you just get a chewer that doesn't care to play with others and just wants to destroy things (our Yuki is a destroyer). It is up to you, the alpha, to provide your destroyer with something you want them to chew on when you are not around. ☺

Soft, Medium and Hard Temperaments

The descriptions below are what we learned during the LER (Littermate Evaluation Report) at about eight weeks of age. This report informs potential dog owners how training should be done and also what *not* do to.

In our Pack, we have Mali, Rani and Yuki which each have a different Temperament. So we get to see how all three handle at once. Not everyone can handle this, so we are not saying try to get one of each. ☺

Mali is a Hard - While she was a Medium during the LER, she has not fooled us and now at three years old, she is more of a hard headed girl than ever. A hard simply means, they can be defiant (talk to the paw, I'm busy right now) and need to be commanded slightly different to get their attention when you need it. A pinch collar may be appropriate for this type of dog.

Yuki is a Medium/Soft - Yes, there are variations of the different Temperaments. Yuki will pay attention to you and do whatever you ask, but if you talk to loudly, it may hurt her feelings. She may also obey a command when you are commanding another dog to do something, like sit or down. She loves attention when she wants it. She also loves to play and do things with you. Sometimes a medium dog needs the choke or pinch collar during training, but rarely should a pinch collar be necessary.

Rani is a Soft - She is always willing to do things for us and loves the attention. She gets jealous when you are giving another dog more attention than her. She will also feel like she is being punished when you command another dog to do something. She will almost always obey the command you are doing to another dog. She has a hard time separating when it is her that needs to listen unless you call her name. Soft dogs should not be handled harshly as their feelings get hurt. A flat collar or choke collar should be fine with this type of dog since they will most often be right at your side and waiting to please you.

Hera is a medium - She does whatever she can do to get your attention. She will wiggle her way into your arms, between your legs and squeeze her long body between you and any other dog getting the attention. Hera always has a smile on her face is just loves to play with the other girls and us. I can even ask her to fight and she will stand up on her hind legs and wrap her front paws around my extended arms and just let me slap her face side to side (in fun of course). When she stands up (10 months old mind you), she is already taller than I am. She is the first to alert, first to howl (she just loves to howl) and tries to be first in and outside.

Pet, Breed or Show Quality

During the LER, the tester will determine whether the puppy will be a Pet, good for Breeding or Showing. There are a number of tests that are administered to help with this determination, along with your feedback on their behaviors during their first eight weeks of life. When a breeder sells a puppy, it will be considered a Pet, Breed or Show quality. Each one identifies how much it will cost to purchase the puppy based on the breed founders set rates.

Pet Upgradable or Pet-Up

There may be times where it is harder to tell for a variety of reasons if the puppy will be good for breeding or showing, so it will be sold as Pet-Upgradable. This means you pay the Pet price, but if a decision is made the puppy can be bred or shown, you pay the difference between the Pet and breed/show price when that time comes.

CHAPTER **13**

Puppy Adoptions &
Finding a Breeder

Pre-Adoption Puppy Application

Here is a copy of our Pre-Adoption Puppy Application. This information along with conversations and meetings between the prospective new owner and the breeder will determine which puppy is best for that home. The details provided are used to help match your lifestyle with that of your potential new puppy's personality.

Madden's Shilohs Kennel

MSK_pre-adoption_application_rev1.doc June 2009

ISSR SHILOH SHEPHERDS™
PRE-ADOPTION APPLICATION FOR PUPPIES

Check, circle all that applies and print clearly. Thank You.

1. **I would like a:** a) male   b) female   c) either

2. **I would like a:** a) sable   b) dual   c) no color preference

3. **The temperament I expect from my dog, as per the following possibilities would be:**
   The mailman knocks at the door with a package delivery, I want my dog to:
   a) bark, then make friends
   b) bark, then chew him up
   c) bark, and not make friends
   d) other: _____

4. **My dog and I are taking a walk in the park and I see some old friends. I want my dog to:**
   a) wag his tail
   b) attack them
   c) ignore them
   d) other: _____

5. **In what type of housing do you reside?**
   Apt/condo   Town House   Single Family

6. **Do you live in the**   city   farm/ranch   small town
   how many acres_____

7. **Do you own rent?** If you rent, does the landlord permit large dogs?   Yes   No

8. **Would you permit us to contact your landlord?** Yes   No
    Landlord's name/phone number _____

9. **Do you have a fenced yard?**   **Yes   No**
    If yes, type and height of fence _____

10. **My dog will spend most of his time:**
    a) in the house
    b) in a kennel run
    c) running loose
    d) in the fenced yard
    e) on a chain
    f) other: _____

11. **How many hours of the day would the dog normally be left alone?** _____

12. **Which family member will have the major responsibility for the dog?** _____

13. **I am interested in training my dog in:**
    obedience   search & rescue/herding   Schutzhund
    agility   therapy/seeing eye   other: _____

14. **I am interested in show and/or breeding:**   Yes   No

15. **I am interested in a pet & plan to spay/neuter:** Yes   No

16. **Are you willing to have your dog's hips x-rayed (OFA, OVC or PennHip) at the age of 12-14 months and provide us with the report?** Yes   No

17. Do you have a current veterinarian and if so, may we contact him/her? Yes   No

Provide contact info for veterinarian _____

_____

18. My experience with large breed dogs is I:
   a)   never owned a large dog
   b)   had a large dog growing up as a family pet
   c)   have owned a large dog in the past and am confident in my ability to handle/train one
   d)   am an experienced trainer/handler of large dogs

19. I have owned _____ dogs in the past _____ years

20. My dogs:
were given away   were euthanized because _____
were killed in accidents   died of old age
other: _____

21. My household consist of _____ **dogs, (please list age, breed and sex & if spayed/neutered):**_____

22. My household consists of:
___ adults   ___ children (ages) _____
___ cats   ___ birds (type) _____
___ other _____

23. If you do not currently have children, do you expect to have children in the future?   Yes   No

24. The adults in my household are: 0-20   20-30   30-40   40-50   50-60   60 & up

25. Do any members of your household have allergies?   Yes   No
If yes, please list: _____

_____

26. The activities that best describe our lifestyle is:

Couch potato   Relaxed walks – occasionally   daily

Weekend hiker   Daily runner

Marathon runner that can't sit still

27. Please supply two references and contact numbers or e-mail addresses:

Name: _____

Contact #/Email: _____

Name: _____

Contact #/Email: _____

28. Any additional comments you may have, which may help us choose the correct temperament pup for you (ie. Lifestyle: runner, hiker, etc), **would be appreciated:**

_____

_____

_____

_____

_____

Finding a breeder

When you are ready to adopt your first Shiloh Shepherd™, you want to find a breeder that is not only close to you, but one who will be able to answer questions. It is also a good resource to have to find a mentor if you are also going to be a breeder..

The breeder should be a LB (Licensed Breeder) or LBIT (Licensed Breeder In Training) and should be able to provide you with a match for your family. The Pre-Adoption Application helps the breeder to find the right puppy for your family, so it is critical to answer all questions truthfully and accurately. This application and the LER will determine which puppy or puppies are best for you. Chapter 14 has a link to all the Shiloh Shepherd™ Licensed Breeders as well as other important links you may want to visit.

Breeders care about the puppies they are raising and putting up for adoption. If it doesn't work out for whatever reason, you should never put your Shiloh in a shelter. Always, contact the breeder and make arrangements for returning or re-homing your Shiloh. This is part of the agreement when you adopt a Shiloh. We need to do everything possible to ensure he/she has the proper home.

CHAPTER 14

Website Reference Information

Standards and Clubs

Official Shiloh Site - http://www.shilohshepherds.org

Shiloh Shepherd™ Breed Standard - http://www.shilohshepherds.info/standard.htm

Shiloh Shepherd™ Coat Colors - http://www.shilohshepherds.info/issrShilohShepherdsCoatColor.pdf

I.S.S.R. Rules and Regulations - http://www.shilohshepherds.info/issr.htm

Shiloh Shepherd™ Dog Club of America, Inc. - http://www.ssdca.info

Registered Kennel Names - http://www.shilohshepherds.org/issrIncRegisteredKennelNames.htm

Shiloh Shepherd™ Learning Center - http://www.shilohshepherds.info

Our website - http://www.maddenshilohs.com

FDA Pet Food Recall List - http://www.accessdata.fda.gov/scripts/newpetfoodrecalls

About the Breed and Founder

Breed Founder - Tina Barber - http://www.shilohshepherd.com/kennelof.htm

Investigate before you invest - http://www.shilohshepherds.info/investigate.htm

Shiloh Shepherds™, A Breed Under Development - http://www.shilohshepherds.info/tinaBarberShilohShepherdArticle.htm

Who's Who "Real Shiloh Shepherds" - http://www.tinambarber.info/whosWho.htm

Shiloh Shepherd™ Friends Forum - http://www.shilohshepherdfriends.com

Shiloh Shepherd™ Store - http://www.shilohshepherdsinfo.com/shilohStore.htm

Proper Puppy Socializing - http://www.shilohshepherds.info/properSocialization.htm

Other Training Books - http://www.cedarwoods-k9.com/
eisenmann/

Breeding

Licensed Breeder Requirements - http://www.shilohshepherds.
info/appendixA.htm

Licensed Breeder Agreement - http://www.shilohshepherds.
info/licensedBreederAgreement.htm

Breeders Code of Ethics - http://www.shilohshepherds.info/
breedersCodeofEthics.htm

Licensed Breeders - http://www.shilohshepherds.org/licensed-
Breeders.htm

Licensed Breeder Matrix - http://www.shilohshepherds.info/
issrLicensedBreederMatrix.htm

Litter Evaluation Program Manual - http://www.shilohshep-
herds.info/lerManual.htm

Upcoming Litters - http://www.newzionshilohs.org/upcom-
ing_litters.htm

Win Sheets and other Forms

I.S.S.R. Puppy - http://www.shilohshepherds.info/issrShow-
Forms/issrPuppyWinSheetRev203.pdf

I.S.S.R. Adult - http://www.shilohshepherds.info/

issrShowForms/issrAdultwinsheetRev203.pdf

TCCP Reports - http://www.shilohshepherds.info/tccpOrder-Form.htm

Pre-Adoption Application - http://www.maddenshilohs.com/MSK_pre-adoption_application_rev1.pdf

Sales Contract - http://www.maddenshilohs.com/MSK_Sales_Contract_rev1.pdf

Co-Ownership Contract - http://www.maddenshilohs.com/MSK_Co-Ownership_Contract_rev1.pdf

Medical Sources

http://www.PetMD.com

http://www.EntirelyPets.com

Alaska State Public Health Lab

The CDC-DPDx - http://www.dpd.cdc.gov/dpdx/HTML/Image_Library.htm Cuyahoga Falls Veterinary Clinic, Inc. http://fallsvetclinic.com

CPSIA information can be obtained at www.ICGtesting.com
Printed in the USA
BVOW04s0206240314

348567BV00001B/37/P